CHEST

BARBARA CLUFF

Illustrated by

BARBARA AND ROGER CLUFF

ALL RIGHTS RESERVED
Text copyright © Barbara Cluff 2024
Cover illustration & illustrations
© Barbara and Roger Cluff 2024

ISBN 978-1-0686854-0-8

The right of Barbara Cluff to be identified as the author of this work, as well as the right of Barbara and Roger Cluff to be identified as the illustrators of this work, has been asserted by them in accordance with the Copyright, Designs and Patents Act 1988.

This edition first published by BEEKABAA in the UK 2024
Email: barbara@beekabaa.co.uk

This book is sold subject to the condition that it shall not, by way of trade or otherwise, be lent, re-sold, hired out, or otherwise circulated in any form of binding or cover other than that in which it is published. No part of this publication may be reproduced, stored in a retrieval system, or transmitted in any form or by any means – including, but not by way of limitation, graphic, electronic or mechanical, including photocopying, recording, taping – without the prior permission, in writing, of the copyright owner.

A CIP catalogue record for this book is available at the British Library.

Book typeset by The Better Book Company
and printed by Imprint Digital.

AUTHOR'S NOTE
This book is a revised version of Cartwheeling Chestie Nut.

CONTENTS

Chapter   Page

THE FIRST BOOK

1. Coming Down The Tree 1
2. Mr Rain And The Solar Alien 4
3. Meeting Chris 8
4. Chris's Birthday 12
5. The Magic Word 17
6. Paul Peck 21
7. A Present For Mum 26

THE SECOND BOOK

8. The First Day At School 31
9. The Alphabet Tree 34
10. A Red Squirrel Turns Into A Grey Squirrel 38
11. A Cap 42
12. Reading Homework 45
13. The Perfect Store For Nuts 50
14. Tracking The Monster 53
15. GreyGory 56
16. On The Way To The Green Island 60
17. Nicholas Adrian 63

Chestie's Song

INTRODUCTION

Chestie Nut, a little red squirrel, lived with his family in a pine tree at the edge of the forest. He was very proud of his fur, which was the colour of bright chestnuts.

THE FIRST BOOK

1

COMING DOWN THE TREE

The autumn mist lifted slowly, revealing the waking forest. The first rays of the sun lit up clusters of hazelnuts on the bushes.

'Hurry up, Chestie!' Hazel Nut called. 'Winter's on its way and we're late with burying nuts.'

'It's too early!' Yawning, Chestie Nut stumbled out of the nest and saw his sister running down the tree.

'I'm coming!' he called. Then he looked down and turned pale: 'Oh no! It's so far to the ground! Everything's going round and round.'

'Get out of the way, you big baby!' The other squirrels bumped into him, as they rushed past.

A tear rolled down Chestie's cheek. 'Why can't I be like other squirrels and run down trees?' he sighed. 'Perhaps I'll try.'

He hopped from one leg to the other. 'It's now or never,' he told himself and leapt onto the branch below.

The branch swung backwards and forwards, backwards and forwards, and ... snapped!

'Aaaaah!' Chestie cried as he fell.

He spread out his arms, his legs and his tail.

'Wow, I'm flying!'

He turned a cartwheel in the air –

down he went,

down

and

down ...

'Ooeee!' Chestie squeaked. He burst through some hazelnut bushes, turned head over tail, and then landed softly in the moss.

Hazel pointed at the ground. 'Look at all the nuts you've knocked down!'

'Wow!' he exclaimed. 'I'm a real squirrel now!'

Hazel and Chestie began to bury the nuts.

'Is this my little brother?' Hazel teased.

The other squirrels were amazed. They even said, 'Sorry' to Chestie for calling him a baby.

In the afternoon, Chestie turned cartwheels along a branch. He sang:

'I'm a cartwheeling Chestie Nut,
I'm happy today,
Because now I've come down the tree,
Ho, hum, ho, hey, hey!

I leap from a branch to a branch,
Run down and up trees,
I'm a very proud Chestie Nut,
Ho, hum, ho, hee, hee!'

2

MR RAIN AND THE SOLAR ALIEN

Winter was very hard and very long. It rained all the time. In his dry, warm nest, Chestie Nut dreamt of spring. One morning, a woodpecker woke him up, PECK! PECK! PECK! Excited, Chestie jumped up and ran outside to greet the sun. But it was raining … Plip, plap, plop, plat, plop, plat, plip …

'Oh! Nutty nuts!' he cried and looked up. Plop! A big raindrop splashed his nose. Chestie rubbed his wet nose dry and asked, 'Mr Rain, don't you ever go to sleep?' As it was still raining he decided to sing Mr Rain a lullaby.

He began the first verse:

'Do you want to rain all day?

To spit, splash, spatter and spray,

Through low clouds in the grey sky

Falling down from very high?'

He looked up at the sky again. 'Mr Rain, did you hear my song?'

An even bigger raindrop fell into his ear. 'Ow!' he cried, and tilted his head to let the water run out. Then he sang the second verse:

'Mr Rain, go back to your bed.

Do it quickly, as I said.

Dream of puddles, cool and deep,

They will soon rock you to sleep.'

But Mr Rain was wide awake. Plip, plap, plop, plat, plop, plat, plip!

'I'll be cross with you, Mr Rain!' Chestie wagged a finger and stamped his feet. He sang the third verse:

'I'll sing again and again,

To stop this very wet rain.

Ask the sun, now please be proud

And smile through dense fog and cloud.'

All at once, a shy ray of sunlight came through the clouds. Mr Rain went to bed, so it stopped raining.

'Mr Rain,' said Chestie. 'I hope you won't snore!'

Then he called to his sister who was in the nest, 'Hazel, you can come out now. I've put Mr Rain to bed.'

'How did you do that?' she asked.

'I sang Mr Rain a lullaby!' he boasted.

Hazel's eyes opened wide. 'Did you really???'

'Yes, he did,' said another voice. A voice they didn't recognise.

Astonished, Chestie and Hazel glanced around. A brightly shining creature stood nearby, smiling at them.

'Who are you?' Chestie and Hazel asked together.

'I'm a Solar Alien from the sun,' replied the creature. 'I've been trapped by Mr Rain. Now I can go back home along the rainbow.' He pointed towards the sky.

'Can we come with you?' asked the squirrels.

'No, you can't,' said the creature. 'But I'll leave you this mirror. It will protect you from a monster.'

'A mo ... mo ... monster? What monster?' Chestie and Hazel asked.

But the Solar Alien had gone.

Chestie was very happy because he had put Mr Rain to bed. He turned cartwheels along a branch and sang:

'I'm a drying-off Chestie Nut,
It's sunny today,
'Cause I've put Mr Rain to bed,
Ho, hum, ho, hey, hey!

I met the Solar Alien,
And he spoke to me,
I'm a very dry Chestie Nut,
Ho, hum, ho, hee, hee!'

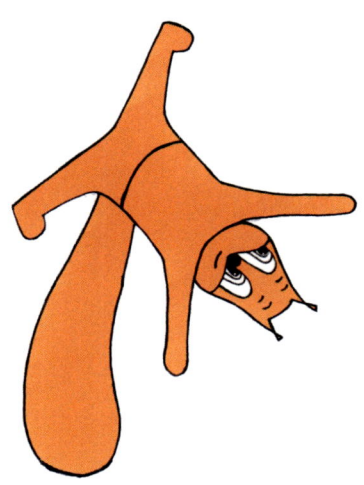

3

MEETING CHRIS

Chestie Nut stood in the sunshine. He held the magic mirror given by the Solar Alien to catch the sunrays. One sunray was reflected down onto the shaded ground next to his sister.

'Hazel,' he said. 'Would you like to play a new game?'

'Yes, I would,' Hazel replied.

'I call this game "Catching The Hare",' he said. 'You can only play it on a sunny day. Do you see the reflected sunray on the ground next to you?'

'Yes.' Hazel nodded. 'I can see its little spot of light.'

'That's The Hare. You have to catch it when I move the mirror.' Chestie moved the mirror and the reflected spot of light moved, too. 'Hazel, catch The Hare!'

Hazel leapt towards it and called, 'I've got it!' But before she could catch The Hare, Chestie moved the mirror and called back to her, 'No, you haven't.'

She followed the spot of light. As Chestie moved the mirror again, the sunray lit up a strange-looking *thing*.

'Hazel, what's that?' he asked.

'I don't know,' she replied. 'Anyway I must go home. Don't be long, Chestie.'

'I won't,' he said. 'But first I must find out what

that *thing* is.' He went up to it and asked, 'Are you a nut?'

The *thing* rolled away and hid under a bush.

Chestie followed. 'Are you a nut?' he repeated.

'Yes,' said a voice from inside the *thing*. 'I'm a lonely coconut.'

'A lonely coconut?' Chestie was amazed.

'Nobody wants to be my friend,' said the voice.

'Well … I'll be your friend.'

'Will you really?' the voice asked. A shutter in the coconut opened with a click. Out came a wood mouse. 'I'm Chris,' he said.

Chestie was even more amazed. 'I'm Chestie,' he said. 'What are you doing in there, Chris?'

'I live here, but it's a secret. Can you keep a secret?'

'Of course,' Chestie promised. 'Has something happened to you?'

'You can never be too cautious in the forest,' said Chris. 'Last night I heard a strange noise so I looked through the keyhole. In the moonlight I saw a huge shadow crossing the path. I froze.'

'What was it?'

'I don't know. Then a cloud covered the moon and everything went dark. I waited for a long time. When it was quiet, I went to bed.'

'Don't worry, Chris,' Chestie said. 'I have this mirror from the Solar Alien.' He held it up. 'It'll protect us from a monster.'

'A mo ... mo ... monster?' Chris stuttered. 'Are you sure that we're safe here?'

'Of course,' Chestie replied. 'Would you like to play a game of "Catching The Hare", Chris?'

'Yes!' Chris said.

Chestie moved the mirror and the reflected sunray lit up a tree stump. Before Chris could catch The Hare, Chestie moved the mirror again. Chris ran after The Hare, time after time, but he never caught up with it. At last, Chestie said to Chris, 'I've won today. We'll play again tomorrow and then we'll see.'

Chris agreed and said, 'And I forgot to tell you, tomorrow is my birthday. Will you come to my party?'

'Of course, I will.'

Later Chestie turned cartwheels along a branch and sang:

'I'm a cartwheeling Chestie Nut,
I'm cheerful today,
Because I have found a friend,
Ho, hum, ho, hey, hey!

I leap from a branch to a branch,
Run down and up trees,
I'm a very smart Chestie Nut,
Ho, hum, ho, hee, hee!'

4

CHRIS'S BIRTHDAY

Next day, Chestie set off for Chris's birthday party. He carried a cake for his new friend. Suddenly he heard, 'HELP, HELP, HELP!' He saw a ladybird drowning in a deep puddle.

He picked up a stick and put it down next to the ladybird. Gasping, she managed to climb out of the water onto it. For a moment, she sat still. Then, 'Thank you for helping me,' she murmured.

'What happened?' Chestie asked.

Mrs Ladybird pointed. 'I was sitting on that flower, when I saw a huge shadow cross the path and come towards me.'

'Was it a mo ... mo ... monster?' Chestie stuttered.

'Perhaps,' she replied. 'He must have brushed against the flower I was sitting on, and I fell into the puddle. Now, I'll grant you a wish because you saved my life.'

'Wow!' Chestie said. 'Any wish?'

'A wish that will help you and will help others, too,' Mrs Ladybird replied and opened her wings.

'Waaait, I don't understand.' Chestie waved his arms, but Mrs Ladybird had gone.

Puzzled, he went on his way.

When he reached Chris's home, the door was open, but there was nobody in. Near the front door there was a bench and a little table. Chestie put the cake on the table and sat down. He sniffed. *Hmmm, the cake smells delicious. I wonder what it tastes like.* He stretched out a finger towards it.

Instantly, a gust of wind whistled past. 'Don't touch the cake,' Mr Wind whispered in Chestie's ear. 'Remember what your mum told you: "NEVER TOUCH FOOD WITH YOUR FINGERS!"'

Chestie paused. 'But I want to taste the cake. Surely it won't matter if I have just a little bit.' He looked around. Nobody was there to see him. So he stuck out his tongue and licked some cream off the cake.

BANG! The cake fell to the ground.

Chestie was horrified. 'What have I done?' he cried out. 'I've ruined Chris's birthday cake!' A moment later, he remembered Mrs Ladybird. 'Mrs Ladybird, Mrs Ladybird,' he called.

Mrs Ladybird landed on his arm almost at once. 'What can I do for you, Chestie?' she asked.

Chestie gazed down at the cake on the ground. 'I didn't touch the cake with my fingers,' he began. 'I touched it with my tongue.' Cream dripped from his chin.

Mrs Ladybird smiled. 'So how can I help?'

'May I have another cake for Chris?'

'Yes, I'll make you another cake.' Mrs Ladybird flew into Chris's kitchen. Soon the oven sang beep, beep and beep. The cake was ready.

Chestie was smiling again. 'Thank you, Mrs Ladybird,' he said.

Mrs Ladybird flew away singing:

'I make people happy,

Even if they're snappy.

I wish them on their way

To have a sunny day.'

When Chris arrived home, Chestie gave him the cake.

'What a lovely cake!' said Chris. 'You've made my day, Chestie!'

Chestie Nut felt happy.

He turned cartwheels along a branch and sang:

*'I'm a cartwheeling Chestie Nut,
I'm friendly today.
I've rescued Mrs Ladybird,
Ho, hum, ho, hey, hey!*

*I leap from a branch to a branch,
Run down and up trees,
I'm a very kind Chestie Nut,
Ho, hum, ho, hee, hee!'*

5

THE MAGIC WORD

While Chestie was exploring the forest, he saw Mrs Ladybird again. 'I know now what you meant the other day,' he said. 'I can only be happy if I'm kind to others!'

'Well done!' Mrs Ladybird praised him.

Chestie was pleased. 'Now,' he said, 'I can feel my tummy rumbling. I wish I had a big, juicy nut salad. If only I knew the magic word …' He paused. 'Mrs Ladybird, do you know the magic word?'

'Yes, I do,' Mrs Ladybird replied, 'but I am not going to tell you. You must find it out for yourself.' And she whizzed away.

As Chestie carried on walking, he noticed a blackbird singing in the branches above his head:

*'A magic word, a magic word,
Twitter tweet, twitter tweed.
When you are in need,
Say the magic word
And you will be heard.'*

'Mrs Blackbird, what is the magic word?' Chestie asked.

17

*'Twitter tweet, twitter tweed,
What a question indeed.'*
Mrs Blackbird trilled and flew away.

Chestie saw the woodpecker's nest. He scampered up the tree to find Mr Peck resting in his armchair.

'Mr Peck, what's the magic word?' Chestie asked.

'What's what?' Mr Peck opened one eye. 'Oh, it's you Chestie. Please come back later.' He closed his eye again and started to snore.

Chestie ran down the tree trunk to the ground. He sat on the grass. *Will I ever find the magic word?* he thought. *Well, I won't stop asking.*

Suddenly, he felt a rush of cold air. A huge shadow moved nearer and nearer as silent wings glided towards him. The sharp claws of an owl snatched his tail and picked him up.

'A MONSTER! HELP!' Chestie screamed and wriggled. But he couldn't escape.

The owl carried him to her nest. 'Here ...' she said to her baby, 'here's a pet for you to play with.'

'Please, please, please, don't give me a squirrel,' the baby owl screeched, and kicked Chestie out of the nest.

'Eeeeee!' Chestie cried as he fell. He turned a cartwheel in the air and landed safely on his feet.

On the way home, he repeated to himself, 'Please! Please! Please?' And all at once, he exclaimed, 'Of course, that's it! "Please" is the magic word!'

At teatime that evening, Mum asked him, 'Chestie, would you like some more nut salad?'

'Yes, *please,*' he replied.

Mum put a large helping on his plate. Chestie ate it up in no time.

After tea, he turned cartwheels along a branch and sang:

'I'm a cartwheeling Chestie Nut,
I'm merry today,
I have found out the magic word,
Ho, hum, ho, hey, hey!

I leap from a branch to a branch,
Run down and up trees,
I can shout out the magic word,
It's PLEASE, PLEASE, PLEASE, PLEASE!'

6

PAUL PECK

On another day Chestie called, 'Mrs Ladybird!'

Mrs Ladybird landed on his nose. 'Good morning,' she said.

'I know the magic word,' Chestie boasted.

'Well …?' she said, waiting.

'It's "*please*"!'

'Well done! And now, you should learn how to behave in the forest.'

'Please tell me.'

'You must always be quiet in case there is a monster around.'

'A mo … mo … monster?' Chestie stuttered. He sat down on the grass and thought about Mrs Ladybird's words. Then, as quietly as could be, he climbed up the pine tree to his nest to have a snooze.

Later, he was snoozing in his warm nest when he heard:

PECK! PECK! PECK!

It woke him up.

'Hmmm … what's that?' Chestie grumbled, surprised. 'I thought we were supposed to be being quiet.'

PECK! PECK! PECK!

Chestie leapt over to the nearby tree where the pecking sound was coming from. There he stopped.

PECK! PECK! PECK!

It was louder now. Chestie glanced over a branch and saw Mr and Mrs Peck and their son Paul. They were teaching Paul to find food. Paul was standing on his head.

'Listen,' said Mr Peck. 'Peck, peck, peck means no food. But pick, pick, pick means there's something hiding under the bark.'

PICK ...!

'See! It's a caterpillar.' And Mr Peck pulled it out.

Paul looked at the caterpillar – and fell out of the nest.

Head first,
down,
down,
and down.

BANG! He landed, with his beak jammed in a cabbage growing under the tree.

'Oh, dear!' Mr Peck exclaimed. As he did so, the caterpillar fell out of his beak and landed on the cabbage next to Paul.

Chestie ran down the tree.

'Paul,' he said. 'Mr Caterpillar can set you free from the cabbage, but you mustn't eat him. Promise?'

'Mmmm,' mumbled Paul.

Mr Caterpillar uncurled himself and began to eat the cabbage round Paul's beak. Crunch, crunch, crunch ... chomp, chomp, chomp ... With each gulp, the hole in the cabbage round Paul's beak grew larger and larger. Deeper and deeper. Soon, Mr Caterpillar had disappeared inside the hole completely!

Chestie took hold of Paul. He pulled, pulled and pulled ... and ... POP! Paul's beak popped out of the cabbage.

'I'm free!' Paul cried, 'but I feel very weak.'
'Have some cabbage salad,' said Mr Caterpillar.
Paul started to peck the cabbage.
'Do you want to be strong and healthy?' Mr Caterpillar asked.
'Mmm,' Paul replied.
'Then, you must eat fruit and vegetables. Five times a day is best,' said Mr Caterpillar.
'I shall,' Paul promised.

Later that day, Chestie went with Paul to see Mr and Mrs Peck.

'From now on,' Paul told his parents, 'I'm going to eat fruit and vegetables. And so should you!'

'But WHY?' Mr and Mrs Peck cried out together.

'Because Mr Caterpillar saved me,' Paul replied. Then he stood on his head again.

Now, I had better leave them, Chestie decided and said 'Bye' to them. Then he looked into all the holes that Mr Peck had made in the tree trunk. He put his finger inside one of them. The hole was deep and round. *I like it*, he thought. *I could hide my nuts here.*

When Chestie got home Hazel asked him, 'Where have you been? I've been looking for you everywhere.'

'Mrs Ladybird told me to be quiet in the forest,' Chestie said. 'So why is Mr Peck so noisy?'

'He's a tree surgeon. He takes care of the trees. Work like that can be noisy.'

Nutty nuts, Chestie thought. *It's all right for some.*

'Tomorrow is Mum's birthday,' Hazel went on. 'What present will you give her?'

'I'll think of something.'

'Don't forget.'

'I won't,' he promised.

Chestie turned cartwheels along a branch. He sang:

'I'm a cartwheeling Chestie Nut,
I'm helpful today,
And I've rescued the woodpecker,
Ho, hum, ho, hey, hey!

I leap from a branch to a branch,
Run down and up trees,
I'm a jolly good Chestie Nut,
Ho, hum, ho, hee, hee!'

7

A PRESENT FOR MUM

It was a sunny morning and it was Mum's birthday. Chestie was looking for a present for her. He skipped down a country lane. Then he stopped and sniffed.

'What is that lovely smell?'

'Go straight on ...' whispered Mr Wind.

Chestie kept walking until he came to a beautiful white flower. It was growing under a bush.

'That's it!' he exclaimed. 'I'll take some flowers for Mum!' But as he bent down to pick the flower, a black, buzzing *thing* flew past his nose.

'What's that?' He swung his arms about to keep the *thing* away.

'Buzz, buzz, buzz!' It came closer.

'Go away, you horrible *thing*!' he shouted.

'Buzz, buzz, buzz! Leave my flowers alone!' the *thing* snapped at Chestie, and it sat on his nose.

'Don't annoy a busy bumble bee,' whispered Mr Wind.

Chestie swatted at the bee.

'Ha, ha, ha! Catch me if you can!' The bee flew straight at Chestie. Then it swerved to the right, flying from one flower to another.

'I'll catch you later,' Chestie said. 'Right now I must pick flowers for Mum.' He set off once more, going deeper and deeper into the woods.

'Don't go too far,' Mr Wind whispered to him again. But Chestie didn't listen.

After a while he decided, 'That will do.' In his paw he held a bunch of pretty white flowers.

He wiped the other paw across his forehead. *It's very hot today*, he thought. *I'll rest here under this oak tree for a while.* He sat down and fell asleep ...

All at once –
CRASH!

A loud thunder-clap woke Chestie up. He jumped up to his feet and looked around. The sun had gone. It was now dark in the forest.

CRASH, BANG!

Thunder rolled right above his head. Then the first raindrops fell into his eyes.

'Oh, oh, oh, a monster!' Chestie cried, and he grabbed the flowers. He ran to the right. He ran to the left. But he didn't know the way home!

Suddenly, he heard a buzzing noise. Something black whizzed past his nose.

'Oh, it's you, the *thing*!'

The *thing*, or rather the bumblebee, was heavy with pollen. It buzzed, 'I must get home and out of the storm. Buzz, buzz, buzz!'

'Wait for me!' Chestie ran after the bee.

'Follow me, child!' buzzed the bee. 'There's going to be a whizz-buzz!'

Chestie chased after the bee, who led him all the way home. When they were there, Chestie asked, 'Who are you?'

'I'm Herbert, a busy bumblebee.'

'I thought you were my enemy!'

'I'll tell you a secret,' said Herbert. 'You never know who will help you. You never know who will be your friend.' And away he flew, back to his home.

Chestie looked down at the one flower still in his paw. He had lost all the others on his way back. He gave that flower to Mum. She was very happy.

'Now, Chestie, come and sit down next to me,' Mum told him. 'I've something important to tell you.'

'Yes, Mum,' Chestie said.

'Listen carefully.' She looked at him. 'Tomorrow will be your first day at school.'

'Do I have to go to school?' he asked, avoiding her eyes.

'Yes, you do,' she said.

Chestie wasn't sure he wanted to.

But later, he forgot what Mum had told him. He turned cartwheels along a branch and sang:

'I'm a cartwheeling Chestie Nut,
I'm joyful today,
I've a lovely gift for Mummy,
Ho, hum, ho, hey, hey!

I leap from a branch to a branch,
Run down and up trees,
I'm a very nice Chestie Nut,
Ho, hum, ho, hee, hee!'

THE SECOND BOOK

8

THE FIRST DAY AT SCHOOL

Early in the morning Mum took Chestie to school. It wasn't far away, under an old barn at the edge of the forest. He saw a group of timid-looking pupils who stood under a sign: YEAR 1.

'Wait here,' Mum said. 'Miss Brown will pick you up.' And she went home.

Chestie looked at the strange faces of the various animals around him. It was a big crowd. *I don't know anybody here*, he thought. *It's scary.*

Then he noticed a teacher approaching the group. *This must be Miss Brown,* he thought. The teacher's stern face, the large glasses on her nose and the ruler in her hand made him feel uneasy.

'Year 1, I am your teacher – Miss Brown,' she said, smiling. 'Follow me.'

She made her way to the classroom. Chestie dawdled along behind the other pupils and sat down at the last desk.

'Today,' said Miss Brown, 'we will learn the first letter of the alphabet.' She wrote an A on the board. 'Repeat after me – A IS FOR APPLE.'

The class repeated.

'Louder!' she said.

'A IS FOR APPLE,' they said.

'No, no, no!' The teacher pointed at the board with her ruler. 'All of you together. Again.'

Chestie felt Miss Brown's eyes watching him. He hid behind a tall pupil sitting in front of him.

Miss Brown beat out the rhythm of the words on the table with the ruler, 'A IS FOR APPLE!'

Perhaps she'll hit me, Chestie thought. *I don't like it here at all.* He waited for the lunchtime bell, and then he ran home.

'I'm not going back to school,' he told Mum. 'I don't know anybody there.'

'Chris and Paul Peck go to school, too,' Mum said. 'They'll have gone home for lunch, so you can go back with them.'

Chestie wasn't sure. But after lunch, Chris and Paul collected Chestie and they returned to school together.

That afternoon, the class started to learn the Alphabet Song. Chestie really enjoyed it. He wasn't scared anymore.

Miss Brown watched him after school. She was pleased to see he was going home with friends.

Chestie turned cartwheels along a branch and sang:

'I'm a cartwheeling Chestie Nut,
I'm at school today,
I have just learned the letter A,
Ho, hum, ho, hey, hey!

I leap from a branch to a branch,
Run down and up trees,
I'm a very good Chestie Nut,
Ho, hum, ho, hee, hee!'

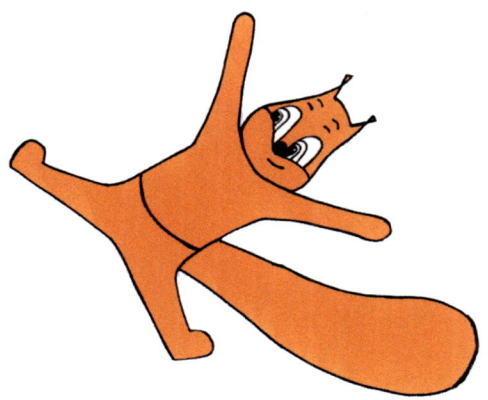

9

THE ALPHABET TREE

'Miss told us today to learn the alphabet at home.' Chestie picked up a plastic letter from the pile and said:

'A is for APPLE.
C is for CAT.
H is for HARE.'

He repeated the letters again and again. But he could only remember C for CAT and H for HARE.

'If only it was easy to learn the alphabet,' he said.

A passing magpie chuckled. 'Hee, hee, hee! Look for the Alphabet Tree.'

'The Alphabet Tree?' Chestie looked puzzled. 'Wait for me!' And he ran after the magpie.

They came to a high wall. Chestie listened. From behind the wall came the sound of voices.

'Wow! I can hear trees telling stories,' he said. There was a gate in front of him, but it was locked. 'If only I could get in there.'

'Hee, hee, hee! Use the key.' The magpie chuckled again, and a golden key fell from his beak. Chestie picked it up and opened the gate.

Instantly, an owl appeared.

'TOO-WIT! TOO-WOO!' Mrs Owl toowitted, flapping her wings. 'TOO-WIT! TOO-WOO!' Her wings were so wide that she looked very, very large.

'A mo ... mo ... monster?' Chestie stuttered.

'TOO-WIT! TOO-WOO! To come into the Magic Garden, you must first spell out your name.'

Behind Mrs Owl, Chestie saw a tree covered with leaves shaped like letters.

'What's the first letter of your name?' asked Mrs Owl.

'It ... it ... it's C,' he muttered, trembling.

As soon as he'd said it, a letter C floated down from the tree. It landed on the ground in front of him.

Mrs Owl asked, 'What's the second letter?'

'It's H.'

A letter H floated down from the tree.

'What's the third letter?'

Chestie didn't know what to say. C and H were the only letters he could remember. He felt like crying.

'We'll say the alphabet together,' Mrs Owl suggested.

Chestie did his best to say the letters along with her:

'A B C D E F G H I J K L M N O P Q R S T U V W X Y Z.'

The Alphabet Tree then dropped the letters to spell:
C H E S T I E   N U T

'Is this my name?' He stared, stared and stared.

'Yes, it is.' Mrs Owl smiled. 'Now you may come into the Magic Garden and help yourself to some lovely hazelnuts. And next time you come, you will need to spell a different word.'

I'll keep these nuts in my old stores, Chestie decided. *And I'll count them every day.* When he reached the first store, he asked himself, 'Has anybody been here? Are there some nuts missing? I'm not sure. Perhaps I'll come here again, tomorrow.'

I know now that I must learn to spell, he thought on

the way home. *Then I can have ripe juicy nuts from the Magic Garden.*

Chestie turned cartwheels along a branch. He sang:

'I'm a cartwheeling Chestie Nut,
I'm spelling today,
And I have learnt the alphabet,
Ho, hum, ho, hey, hey!

I leap from a branch to a branch,
Run down and up trees,
I'm a very keen Chestie Nut,
Ho, hum, ho, hee, hee!'

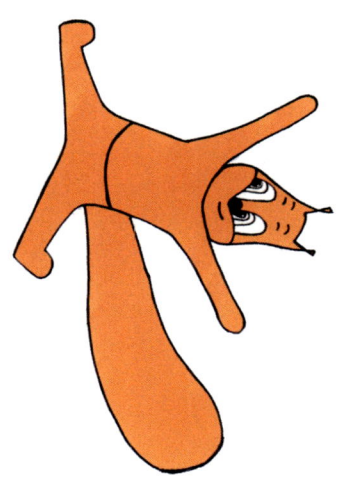

10

A RED SQUIRREL TURNS INTO A GREY SQUIRREL

In the morning Chestie checked over his stores of nuts. *All my nuts are safe*, he thought, satisfied, and went to school.

On the way he came across a very large red *something*. It was turning round and round. *How exciting!* Chestie thought, and he stopped to watch.

One man was feeding the *something* with brown stuff. Grey sludge, like sloppy porridge, flopped out into a wheelbarrow. Another man took the wheelbarrow away.

I must find out what it is, Chestie thought.

The school bell started to ring, but he didn't hear it. He hid under a large leaf, and waited and waited.

At last, the two men wandered off and left the *something* alone.

'Oh, they've forgotten to turn it off,' Chestie said. 'It's now or never!' He jumped out from under the leaf onto the *something*. But it was still turning round and round.

'Ow!' he squeaked. 'It's a monster!' But it was too late. Round and round he went. He tried to jump off, but he tripped – and fell deep into the *something's* big, gaping mouth. Inside, it was completely dark. He was thrown around: *biff-up, bang-down, biff-up, bang-down, biff-up, bang-down.*

'HEEELP!!!' he cried. But nobody heard him.

After a while, the men came back. They turned off the *something* and emptied it.

Chestie flew out and landed on the grass.

'Look at this,' one of the men said.

'Ha, ha, ha! Is it a grey squirrel?' the other man asked.

Chestie felt as though he was still whizzing round and round. His red fur was covered with grey sludge. 'What is this sloppy stuff?' he whimpered. Then he began to cry.

'Don't worry,' said the men. 'It'll wash off.'

Chestie wasn't so sure. Feeling very uncomfortable, he slowly stumbled to school.

'Is that you, Chestie?' Miss Brown asked him. 'You're late. Where have you been?'

'Oh, Miss, the red *something* nearly killed me,' Chestie spluttered. 'It swallowed me up. It spun me round inside – round and round. Then it spat me out!'

'What are you talking about?'

'It was on the way to school, Miss.'

Miss Brown looked at Chestie. Her face was stern. 'Well, let that be a lesson for you and everyone else. You must never ever go anywhere near machinery, even if it's not moving!' She wagged her finger at him. 'YOUR SAFETY IS VERY, VERY IMPORTANT!'

'But ...' Chestie began.

'No buts,' Miss Brown snapped.

'What was it?'

'It was a concrete mixer,' she replied. 'Now you'd better go home at once to get cleaned up!'

At home, Mum washed Chestie's fur. When he was red again, he turned cartwheels along a branch and sang:

'I'm a cartwheeling Chestie Nut,
I'm safe now today,
I've escaped the red mixer,
Ho, hum, ho, hey, hey!

I leap from a branch to a branch,
Run down and up trees,
I'm a very red Chestie Nut,
Ho, hum, ho, hee, hee!'

11

A CAP

Next morning, Chestie said the alphabet to himself while he was cleaning his ears. *Today I'll learn to spell nutty nuts,* he decided. 'N ... n ... n ... It's very difficult.'

Suddenly he paused. 'Hmmm ...' He looked in his mirror. 'There's my left ear ...' He turned his head. 'Now there's my right ear ...' He turned his head again. 'Is my left ear shorter?'

Chestie took a ruler out of his schoolbag.

'First my right ear,' he said and put the ruler against it. He marked an R on the ruler where the tip of his right ear reached.

'Now my left ear ...' He put the ruler against his left ear and marked an L on it where his left ear reached.

'NUTTY NUTS!' He stood with his mouth wide

open as he stared at the two marks. 'Hazel!' he cried out. 'My left ear is shorter than my right ear!'

Hazel was making a red dress in the kitchen. Chestie ran downstairs to find her.

He stopped in front of his sister. 'Look at me. What do you see?'

Hazel glanced at him. 'I see your cheeky face, Chestie.'

'What about my ears?'

'What about them? They look fine to me.'

'Oh no,' he said. 'My left ear is shorter than my right ear.' *Couldn't she see?*

He showed her the ruler. 'This is my right ear. That is my left ear!'

'Ha, ha, ha,' laughed Hazel. She laughed so hard that tears sprang into her eyes.

'Please measure my ears, Hazel.' Chestie jumped towards her.

'Well, Chestie, I think your ears are lovely. They give you character,' she said.

'What's character?' he asked, puzzled.

'It means you're special,' she replied. 'You can hear music in the trees and can sing songs.' Hazel smiled at him. 'And you are the only one of us who turns cartwheels.'

Chestie made a long face. 'But I don't want to be different.'

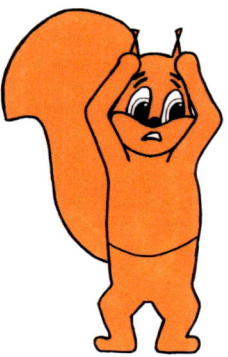

Hazel put her arm round him. 'If you like, I'll make you a cap.' She pointed at the red fabric on the table.

'Yes, please.' Smiling again, Chestie ran outside to play.

When he got back that afternoon, he saw a red cap with a brown peak on his chair. His eyes lit up. 'Is that for me, Hazel?'

Hazel nodded. 'Yes, try it on.'

Chestie put on the cap. He pulled it to one side and looked in the mirror.

'You look lovely,' said Hazel. 'Now, listen.' She gazed into his eyes and sounded very serious. 'I must tell you about the monster that's been seen. Mr Peck and Chris only saw him a long way off. But then Mrs Ladybird saw him near here. And I think I've seen him, too. You must be very careful when you go out. Remember to be quiet.'

'If the monster comes close by, I'll pull my cap right down over my eyes,' Chestie said. 'Then he won't be able to see me. Anyway I'm not afraid of him.'

Chestie turned cartwheels along a branch and sang:

*'I'm a cartwheeling Chestie Nut,
I'm bouncy today,
And I've learnt that I am special,
Ho, hum, ho, hey, hey!*

*I leap from a branch to a branch,
Run down and up trees,
I've a red cap with a brown peak,
Ho, hum, ho, hee, hee!'*

12

READING HOMEWORK

On a windy afternoon Chestie leant over his schoolbook, slowly putting the words together. 'Miss said I have to read at home every day!'

He asked Mr Wind:

'Do I have to learn to read? It's very hard indeed!'

Mr Wind replied:

'Wee-oosh, wee-oosh,
When you are in need
It pays off to be able to read.
Wee-oosh, wee-oosh.'

A moment later, Mr Wind tore Chestie's cap off his head.

'NUTTY NUTS!' Chestie shouted, chasing after it. The cap disappeared over a fence. A big sign said: STRICTLY PRIVATE. Chestie didn't stop to try to read it.

He jumped over the fence. His cap was lying on the grass near a patio. He hopped over to pick it up. But a shadow fell upon him and everything went dark ...

A monster, Chestie thought, terrified. He was caught under a big straw hat. Then he heard a man's angry voice: 'I've got you at last, you little thief! You've been stealing my walnuts.'

'Please let me out, sir!' Chestie cried.
'You've mistaken me for somebody else, sir!'

'In that case, what are you doing here?' the voice asked.

'Mr Wind carried my cap to your garden, sir – and I followed it.'

'I don't believe you! You'll have to prove it!'

Chestie looked through a hole in the hat and said, 'Sir! My cap is over there!'

Suddenly, the front doorbell rang. Chestie heard the man's footsteps as he walked away. Then he heard them come back. The man's voice sounded agitated when he asked, 'Where are my glasses? I can't read this letter from the postman without them.'

'I'll read it for you,' said Chestie quietly.

'Can you read?' asked the voice.

'I'll try, sir,' replied Chestie.

There was a pause. Then the straw hat was lifted and Chestie was able to come out. He saw the man holding the letter. The man looked worried.

'Please.' He gave the letter to Chestie.

Chestie started reading, very slowly:

'Deeer Mun ... mun ... mun ... kle Ccc .. ooo ... mmme ... to ... my ... r ... e ... d ... d ... i ... n ... g ... on ttthe ... sev ... e ... enth S ... t ... a ... r ... ch.

Ben'

'Ah! This is an invitation to my nephew's wedding. It's on the seventh of March.' The man cheered up instantly. 'I'm amazed such a little fellow can read! What's your name?'

'Chestie Nut,' replied Chestie.

'I'm Sir Fuzzy,' the man introduced himself. 'And here's a treat for you.'

He gave Chestie some ripe walnuts. Chestie filled his cap with them. *I'll keep these nuts in my nest, just in case,* he thought.

Then he asked, 'Have you seen the monster, sir?'

'No, I haven't, but I've heard of him.'

'Perhaps he took your walnuts,' suggested Chestie.

'Maybe you're right.'

'Bye, Sir Fuzzy,' said Chestie, and he went home.

'Bye, Chestie.'

On the way home, Chestie said to Mr Wind, 'Now I know why I must learn to read. It'll help me when I'm trapped.'

He turned cartwheels along a branch and sang:

*'I'm a cartwheeling Chestie Nut,
I'm learning today,
And I've read the invitation,
Ho, hum, ho, hey, hey!*

*I leap from a branch to a branch,
Run down and up trees,
I'm a very bright Chestie Nut,
Ho, hum, ho, hee, hee!'*

13

THE PERFECT STORE FOR NUTS

Autumn is here again, Chestie thought. *I'll have to bury more nuts for winter. I'd better check on all my nut stores.*

He came to the first store of nuts. 'OHHH! It's empty!' he cried.

He ran to the next store. 'Nothing here either …!'

He ran further into the forest. '… Or here!'

Startled, he yelled, 'NUTTY NUTS! ALL MY NUTS HAVE GONE!'

Chestie sat down on the grass. *Who could have done this?* he wondered. *If only I had a store that nobody else could find!*

Chris came along. 'What are you doing, Chestie?' he asked.

'I'm thinking.'

'What about?'

'Someone has stolen my nuts,' Chestie said. 'Have you seen anybody?'

Chris frowned. 'In the moonlight, I did see a huge shadow among the trees. And there was a green light searching the ground.' Chris lowered his eyes. 'I hid in my coconut.'

'Nutty nuts!' said Chestie. 'What happened next?'

'I saw a huge paw. It grabbed at the coconut. My coconut was rolled over and over. Inside, I was thrown all over the place. I could not escape.'

'Who was it?' Chestie asked.

'The mo ... mo ... monster,' Chris whispered, trembling. 'I'm sure now.'

'Hmm,' said Chestie. 'Well, I'll have to track him down later. Right now, I need to find a safe hiding place for the nuts Sir Fuzzy has given me.'

Chris pointed at the coconut. 'You can hide them here. I'm moving out.'

'Is it a safe place?' Chestie asked.

'We'll hide the coconut under that bush over there.' Chris pointed towards a thick, low bush. 'Nobody will see it there.'

That afternoon, Chestie turned cartwheels along a branch. He sang:

'I'm a cartwheeling Chestie Nut,
I'm witty today,
I have found a perfect hiding place,
Ho, hum, ho, hey, hey!

I leap from a branch to a branch,
Run down and up trees,
I'm a very quick Chestie Nut,
Ho, hum, ho, hee, hee!'

14

TRACKING THE MONSTER

It had rained all night. In the morning, Chestie's tummy was rumbling.

I'll have a lovely breakfast, he thought on the way to the coconut. But when he reached the thick, low bush the coconut had gone!

'YOU HORRIBLE MONSTER! I'LL FIND YOU ONE DAY, YOU'LL SEE!' he yelled. But although Chestie searched for signs of his enemy, the overnight rain had washed away any tracks.

Chestie wandered on through the forest looking for a new hiding place for his nuts. He heard a twig crack behind him and glanced back. *Is somebody following me?* He paused for a moment, and shook his head. *It's only the wind,* he thought, and went on his way.

By now it had stopped raining and the sun came out. Chestie played with his mirror in the bright light. As he moved it, a reflected sunray lit up a hole in the tree above his head.

'I see Mr Peck has been pecking here, and there, and over there,' he said. 'I'll gather more nuts and hide them in those holes.' And off he went.

Later, he went back to check his new stores.

The first hole was empty. The second hole was empty too. All his new stores were empty!

'NUTTY NUTS!' Chestie yelled. 'ALL MY NUTS HAVE GONE AGAIN!'

He sat down to think. *If only I had a store that nobody else could find!* He looked up and saw Paul Peck land on the tree stump nearby.

'What are you thinking about, Chestie?' Paul asked.

'The monster has found my nuts again. What shall I do?'

'You can hide your nuts in this stump,' Paul replied, and flew away.

Chestie hid the nuts he'd found in the stump and covered them with moss. Nearby, a twig cracked, but this time, he didn't hear it.

Next day, Chestie looked for his nuts, and they had disappeared. Again. Then he noticed Mrs Ladybird crawling out of a puddle.

'What's happened here?' he asked.

'I am sure the monster pushed me in,' Mrs Ladybird said. 'I saw a huge shadow, and a green light searching the ground. I felt ice-cold breath. An enormous paw shot down from above me. Then it vanished. I froze.'

'Which way did the monster go?' Chestie asked.

'I don't know. Perhaps Chris will know. Before, we only saw the monster in the distance. Now, the monster is here,' Mrs Ladybird said. 'He calls himself GreyGory.'

Chestie Nut went to visit Chris in his new home. Chris had moved into an old tree trunk near the school.

'Have you seen GreyGory?' Chestie asked him.

'No,' Chris replied. 'But there are fresh pawmarks in the mud down the path.' He pointed. 'See? They're huge!'

Chestie followed the pawmarks to an oak tree. There they stopped.

'Hey, GreyGory,' he called. 'I can't track you any further. I'm busy now.' And he went back home for lunch. After lunch, Chestie whispered this song:

'I'm a cartwheeling Chestie Nut,
I'm worried today,
And I've tracked down GreyGory,
Ho, hum, ho, hey, hey!

I leap from a branch to a branch,
Run down and up trees,
I'm a very quiet Chestie Nut,
Ho, hum, ho, hee, hee!'

15

GREYGORY

At the end of autumn, GreyGory's squirrels took over the land. The red squirrels hid in the forest and only came out of their nests at night. But Chestie longed to see the sun. So one morning he sneaked out of the nest with his mirror. Hazel tiptoed after him.

Wow! Chestie thought, looking around. *The world is beautiful!* The mist lifted slowly, revealing the waking forest. Silvery flowers, grass and pine trees glittered in the first rays of the sun.

Chestie held up the mirror. A sunray was reflected onto the ground.

'Hazel, catch The Hare,' he whispered to his sister.

'I've got it,' she replied.

'No, you haven't.' He moved the mirror.

The reflected sunray now lit up something in the moss. Hazel followed it and, 'Wow!' she said. 'A golden nut!'

The face of the Solar Alien appeared in the mirror. 'This is my gift to you. Use it wisely,' he said.

Chestie hopped up and down. Accidentally, he pointed the mirror at the trees above.

'OOOOWW!' somebody cried out. There was an icy blast of air and a strange smell.

'It's GreyGory!' Hazel whispered to Chestie. 'You've dazzled him!'

As the sun hid behind a black cloud, it grew dark. A green light began to search the ground. Hazel and Chestie hid inside a hollow tree trunk that lay on its side close by. They sat there for ages, without moving. After a long time, Hazel said, 'The danger is over! Now, you must run away from GreyGory. Will you go to the Green Island to save us?'

Chestie thought for a moment. Then, 'Yes, I'll go!' he said.

'Be careful, GreyGory's spies will be watching you!' Hazel warned him. 'But the golden nut – I think it's a gift to protect you.'

Chestie took the golden nut and set off on his way. As he went, he whispered this song to himself:

'I'm a cartwheeling Chestie Nut,
I'm lucky today,
I have found now the golden nut,
Ho, hum, ho, hey, hey!

I leap from a branch to a branch,
Run down and up trees,
To the safety of Green Island,
Ho, hum, ho, hee, hee!'

16

ON THE WAY TO THE GREEN ISLAND

Chestie rushed as fast as he could to reach the Green Island. In front of him he saw the Squidgy Bog.

'How will I cross that?' he muttered. 'Ah, there are stepping stones.' He cheered up. 'WHEE!' He leapt from one stone to another.

All at once, he heard ... 'Heeelp!'

'Don't look round,' Mr Wind whispered. 'It's GreyGory, trying to catch you.'

But Chestie turned round anyway.

An avalanche of stones, tufts of grass, mud and water was approaching fast. It seemed to be blown by an invisible force.

'Oi, oi, oi!' Chestie screamed.

'Hide in that hole in the bank,' whispered Mr Wind. 'GreyGory has released the Bog Beast!'

Chestie held up his mirror and dazzled the Bog Beast with it. Then he jumped into the hole in the grass. It was so well hidden you could hardly see it. Worn out, he covered himself with his tail and soon fell asleep.

When he woke up, Chestie peered cautiously out of the hole. The Bog Beast had vanished. So Chestie decided it was safe to carry on walking.

'Where are you going?' Up ahead, a Friendly Fairy beckoned to him.

'Don't talk to strangers!' Mr Wind whispered.

Chestie didn't listen. 'I'm on my way to the Green Island.'

'WHAT?' the Fairy yelled. She didn't look friendly anymore and stretched out sharp claws towards him.

'NUTTY NUTS!' Chestie called out and ran for his life towards the river.

Loose screws, tins, nails, door handles and computers jangled behind him. He turned round. The Fairy had changed into the Metal Giant. Again, Chestie held up his mirror to dazzle his enemy. *If only I could cross the river!* He leapt with all his might ... and landed on the other side. Although he was now on the Green Island he still wasn't safe. GreyGory was following him.
In the distance, Chestie saw a small cottage. *I'll hide there*, he decided. On the way he whispered:

'I'm a cartwheeling Chestie Nut,
I'm winning today,
Against all of GreyGory's spies,
Ho, hum, ho, hey, hey.

I leap from a branch to a branch,
Run down and up trees,
I'm a very brave Chestie Nut,
Ho, hum, ho, hee, hee.'

62

17

NICHOLAS ADRIAN

It was Christmas on the Green Island. Nicholas Adrian awoke with a start. 'I'll tiptoe downstairs to see my presents,' he said. Just then he noticed a brown paper parcel on his bed. One corner was already open. Nicholas peered inside. A pair of black eyes looked straight back at him. A voice said, 'Hide me!'

Surprised, Nicholas asked, 'Who are you?'

'Hide me, quickly!'

The boy tucked the parcel

under his pillow and sat on the bed, puzzled. A large shadow crossed the window. The bedroom went dark and a green light began to search the floor. Nicholas covered his head with a blanket and shut his eyes tight.

WHACK! The window burst open and in floated a strange smell. The floorboards began to creak. An icy breath of air shot through the room. Nicholas froze. After a very, very long time, all went quiet. From under his pillow, a muffled voice said, 'It's over now. Let me out!'

Nicholas lifted the pillow slowly. A red squirrel jumped out of the parcel and said, 'I've escaped from GreyGory again!'

'Who are you?' asked Nicholas.

'I'm Chestie Nut,' the red squirrel introduced himself. 'I'm running away from GreyGory, who is the enemy of the red squirrels and other animals.'

Nicholas Adrian thought for a moment. 'We'll set a trap for him,' he said.

'How?' asked Chestie.

'Just wait ...' Nicholas had a spaceship. He filled it with cashew nuts, and put it outside the window.

They smell delicious, Chestie thought.

Nicholas Adrian and Chestie Nut waited and waited.

At last, everywhere went dark again. Then there came that strange smell. Outside, the green light moved around, and GreyGory climbed into the spaceship.

BANG! The hatch slammed shut. Instantly, the green light disappeared. With a ROAR and a WHOOOSH the spaceship took off. It whizzed far away from the earth.

GreyGory's squirrels followed him. And they were never seen again.

All the red squirrels and all the other animals cheered when they heard the news. They raced to the Green Island and danced in a circle round Chestie Nut and Nicholas Adrian.

Chestie Nut turned cartwheels and sang at the top of his voice:

*'I'm a cartwheeling Chestie Nut,
I'm blissful today,
Because GreyGory's gone away,
Ho, hum, ho, hey, hey!*

*I leap from a branch to a branch,
Run down and up trees,
I'm a very free Chestie Nut,
Ho, hum, ho, hee, hee!'*